Original title:
Emotional Algebra

Copyright © 2024 Creative Arts Management OÜ
All rights reserved.

Author: Lila Davenport
ISBN HARDBACK: 978-9916-90-634-7
ISBN PAPERBACK: 978-9916-90-635-4

The Algorithm of Affection

In a world of code and light,
Hearts connect with pure delight.
Numbers dance in soft embrace,
Love's logic finds a sacred place.

Binary whispers, soft and clear,
In every byte, I sense you near.
Emotions coded, deep and wise,
In every spark, affection lies.

Patterns form in every glance,
A symphony of fate and chance.
As algorithms weave their thread,
Our stories bloom, our futures spread.

Yet in the data, one must find,
The warmth of love, a rare design.
Beyond the screen, our hearts will soar,
Together, forever, we explore.

Calculating Heartbeats

In quiet moments, I count the beats,
Each thud a whisper, where love repeats.
A rhythm steady, through joy and pain,
In time with you, my heart's refrain.

Days add up in a gentle sway,
Feelings multiply, come what may.
In shadows cast by our laughter's song,
Every heartbeat brings us along.

The Equation of Feelings

Love is a sum we may never explain,
A mix of pleasure, a dash of pain.
We solve for the joy in a fleeting glance,
X marks the spot where hearts dare to dance.

Variables changing with each passing light,
Like stars that blink in the deep of the night.
We plot our graph on this canvas of fate,
Finding our roots as we patiently wait.

Variables of the Soul

In the chambers of the heart, equations unfold,
With every secret, a mystery told.
The variables shift as we learn and grow,
In the garden of life, our truths overflow.

Each thought a number, each feeling a sign,
Balancing chaos in a world so divine.
Together we laugh, together we cry,
In the math of our souls, we reach for the sky.

Balance of Brokenness

In shattered pieces, a beauty revealed,
Each crack a story, a heart that's healed.
We search for the weight, the scale of our pain,
In the balance of brokenness, hope will remain.

With every fracture, a lesson endures,
Building foundations from what life secures.
Embracing our flaws, we find we are whole,
In the dance of our hearts, we embrace our soul.

Fractions of Longing

In silent whispers, hearts collide,
Fragments of dreams, we cannot hide.
Each moment, a piece, so bittersweet,
In the dance of time, our souls meet.

Ghosts of wishes linger near,
Shadows of hope, a soft veneer.
Through tangled paths, we weave and roam,
Seeking in fragments, a place called home.

Solving for Joy

In every equation, a spark resides,
Solving for joy, where love abides.
Variables shift, and angles bend,
Finding the light where shadows end.

A smile's quotient, the laughter's sum,
In gentle moments, we become.
Through trials and tests, we strive to see,
The solution lies in harmony.

The Derivative of Loss

With every goodbye, the heart computes,
The essence of love in fading roots.
Calculating pain, learning the cost,
Taking the measure of what is lost.

In the graphs of memory, valleys align,
Each dip and rise, by design.
Yet through the sorrow, a truth is found,
In the measures of love, we are unbound.

Adding Up Memories

In the ledger of time, we tally the days,
Each memory, a treasure, in countless ways.
Moments like raindrops, they shimmer and fall,
Adding up laughter, embracing it all.

With every sunbeam, we inscribe our fate,
Counting the blessings, we navigate.
Together we stand, as histories blend,
In the sums of our lives, love will transcend.

Equations of Empathy

In the heart, we find the sum,
Two souls connect, a gentle hum.
Variables of pain and joy,
Together we mend, never to destroy.

Each tear, a fraction of our strain,
With kindness, we solve the pain.
Our stories weave in tender grace,
Empathy, a warm embrace.

Tangents of Triumph

In every struggle, angles change,
Through storms of doubt, we rearrange.
A path once steep begins to rise,
With courage found, we touch the skies.

Momentum builds, the drive ignites,
In dreams pursued, we reach new heights.
The curve of effort bends our way,
In shared success, we brightly sway.

The Proof of Us

In every glance, a theorem lies,
Together, we can defy the skies.
Each moment shared, a step we take,
In love's embrace, no hearts can break.

Through challenges, we must insist,
The bonds we forge can't co-exist.
Our journey, marked by every trust,
In every trial, it's proof of us.

The Slope of Solitude

In quiet corners, whispers dwell,
A lonely path, no stories tell.
Each step a downhill, gradual slide,
Seeking solace, hearts must bide.

Yet in the shadows, light may creep,
In silence, thoughts begin to leap.
The slope may steep, but hope remains,
In solitude, our strength regains.

Dividing Dreams

In the silence, dreams divide,
Whispers echo, hope is tied.
Fragments of a brighter state,
Woven paths we navigate.

In the night, visions call,
Shadows dance, we may fall.
Each step leads us to the light,
A journey born from darkest night.

The Graph of Our Hearts

On paper, lines entwine,
Measured beats, yours and mine.
Data points that intertwine,
Drawing patterns, love aligns.

Through peaks and troughs we roam,
In this chart, we find our home.
Axis shifts, but still we trace,
Every curve a warm embrace.

Correlations of Love

Two hearts beat a steady song,
In rhythms where we both belong.
Connected through unspoken ties,
In every glance, our spirits rise.

Moments shared in sweet refrain,
In laughter's echo, joy and pain.
Together as we chase the stars,
In this dance, love never marred.

Constants in the Chaos

In storms of life, we find our way,
Amid the noise, we choose to stay.
Through swirling doubts, our faith remains,
Holding fast through joys and pains.

In shadows deep, a light will shine,
Our souls, forever intertwined.
With every trial, we grow strong,
In chaos, love will guide along.

Derivatives of Pain

In shadows deep where sorrow dwells,
Each heartache whispers, softly tells.
The curves we trace, our grief's own art,
A calculus of the aching heart.

Through jagged paths we wander lost,
Where each small moment bears its cost.
The limit approaches, pain remains,
In every derivative, memory stains.

Yet in this math, we learn to grow,
From every loss, a seed to sow.
The graph of life, though steep the climb,
Finds strength in struggle, loss in time.

Integrating Hope

In quiet corners, dreams align,
Hope's gentle wave, a sacred sign.
We sum the moments, rich and bright,
An integral of love and light.

Each heartbeat counts, a life defined,
In every struggle, peace we find.
With every breath, new paths we trace,
An integration of the human grace.

From darkness deep, our spirits rise,
The dawn unshackled, open skies.
In unity, we cast away
The shadows of a yesterday.

The Polynomial of Passion

In variables of joy and pain,
We plot our dreams, our hopes remain.
Each term a story, rich and vast,
A polynomial that holds our past.

The roots we seek, in love we bind,
Complex equations, hearts entwined.
With every factor, truth unfolds,
In passion's graph, the future holds.

Through every twist, the lines we draw,
An arc of life, a wondrous flaw.
In passion's blaze, we find our way,
A symmetry that cannot sway.

Imaginary Parts of Us

In realms unseen, where dreams reside,
Imaginary lines, where hearts collide.
The complex truths we hold so dear,
In every whisper, love appears.

Through tangled thoughts, we shape our fate,
With every sigh, we navigate.
The numbers dance in twilight's glow,
A fabric spun of ebb and flow.

In wild equations, love is free,
The imaginary parts of you and me.
Together woven, clear and bright,
Our spirits soar into the night.

The Equation of Longing

In shadows deep, I search for light,
A yearning heart that aches each night.
Each whispered dream a silent plea,
To bridge the gap between you and me.

Moments pass like fleeting smoke,
With every breath, a heartstring broke.
In every echo, your name I find,
An endless riddle of the heart and mind.

Lines of fate draw us apart,
Yet in my core, you share my heart.
The math of love, both sweet and cruel,
A complicated, beautiful rule.

Fractions of Joy

In bits and pieces, happiness gleams,
Like scattered sunbeams in our dreams.
We savor moments, small and bright,
Each fraction sparkles, pure delight.

A laugh shared over coffee's steam,
The warmth of friendship, a gentle beam.
In fleeting seconds, love appears,
Creating memories from laughter and tears.

Though life divides, the joy remains,
In every heart, love spills like rains.
We gather fragments, stitched with care,
A tapestry woven, beyond compare.

Balancing Tears and Laughter

In the scales of life, we weigh each tear,
Against the laughter that brings us near.
With every sorrow, joy shall rise,
Like sunlit clouds in stormy skies.

We dance on edges, a timeless sway,
In bitter moments, we find our way.
Though heart may ache, we learn to play,
A beautiful balance, day by day.

Through trials faced and laughter shared,
We find a strength that's deeply bared.
In mirth and mourning, we learn to cope,
An intricate dance, the thread of hope.

The Sum of Our Silences

In quiet corners, secrets dwell,
Within the silence, stories swell.
The weight of words left unspoken,
Lingering whispers, gentle token.

A gaze that lingers, a touch that stays,
In dusky hours, our hearts display.
With every pause, a deeper truth,
In silent realms, we reclaim our youth.

The sum of us, a quiet spell,
In every silence, we know so well.
Together, not just in loud embrace,
But in the hush, we find our place.

The Rhythm of Reckoning

In shadows deep, the truth will creep,
What lies beneath, we'll start to reap.
With hearts so bold, we step ahead,
To face the past, where fears have tread.

The clock will chime; we cannot wait,
Each tick reveals our hidden fate.
In silence loud, our hopes will grow,
As we embrace the things we know.

A pattern forms in every beat,
We dance with fate, we feel complete.
The choices made, the paths we walk,
In every glance, the echoes talk.

So let the music guide our hands,
As we create our own demands.
The rhythm waits for no retreat,
In unity, we find our feet.

Finding X in Our Hearts

In every puzzle, lies a key,
A simple truth, just you and me.
We'll search together, side by side,
For hidden answers that we hide.

Through tangled paths, we'll make our way,
In quiet moments, come what may.
With every breath, we'll take the chance,
To solve the puzzle of romance.

A whispered dream, a silent vow,
In our shared space, we'll learn somehow.
The missing piece will soon appear,
In love's equation, crystal clear.

So mark the spot where hearts align,
In this grand search, your hand in mine.
Each beat reveals what we can see,
X marks the love that sets us free.

The Limit of Love

Once we reach the edge of trust,
We find the line where dreams combust.
With open hearts, we dance so close,
Yet fear can blur the very most.

Beyond the bounds of what is seen,
A limit lies, both soft and keen.
In every glance, a pull, a sigh,
We question love, we laugh, we cry.

Yet in that space, a choice is made,
To leap, to be, not to evade.
For love's embrace can stretch so wide,
Beyond the fears that we confide.

So let us draw our lines with care,
With boundaries forged, but love laid bare.
In every limit, something new,
A universe, just me and you.

Intervals of Intimacy

In fleeting moments, time escapes,
Where silence weaves its softest tapes.
Each stolen glance, a world unveiled,
In brief embrace, a bond we've sealed.

The space between, a subtle line,
Where hearts collide, where souls entwine.
A gentle touch beneath the stars,
In every beat, love heals our scars.

Amid the chaos, we find peace,
An interval where fears release.
In whispered words, we share our dreams,
A sacred space, or so it seems.

So let us cherish every space,
These fragments shared, this loving grace.
In intervals of sweet delight,
We find our home, our guiding light.

The Spectrum of Sentiments

Colors dance within the heart,
Shades of joy and sorrow's art.
Each emotion tells a tale,
In whispers soft or voices pale.

A canvas bright with laughter's hue,
Yet shadows linger, deep and true.
Every feeling has its place,
In life's vast and tender space.

Moments fleeting, fleeting bliss,
Hope and love, we can't dismiss.
Yet in the dark, we find our way,
Through cracks of light, come what may.

So let us paint with all we know,
In every feeling, let love grow.
Embrace the tide of highs and lows,
For in each wave, our spirit glows.

Distributing Kindness

A simple gesture can ignite,
A spark that fills the world with light.
A smile shared with strangers near,
Can brighten days, dissolve the fear.

With gentle words and caring hands,
We build a bridge through life's demands.
Each act of grace, a seed we sow,
In gardens where compassion grows.

Let kindness flow like rivers wide,
Uniting hearts, our humble guide.
In small exchanges, truth reveals,
The magic that our spirit feels.

So let us share, both near and far,
For every soul is a shining star.
In this great dance, we find our worth,
Distributing kindness, healing Earth.

The Function of Trust

In fragile bonds, we weave our fate,
A tapestry of love and weight.
Trust is a bridge, both wide and tall,
Holding us through the rise and fall.

With open hearts, we find our ground,
In honesty, our peace is found.
Each promise made, a thread so fine,
Strengthens the ties, makes us align.

Yet trust can break, a fragile glass,
With care and time, we can surpass.
Forgiveness blooms in tender light,
Rebuilding faith with each new night.

Let's nurture roots that intertwine,
For in this space, we'll brightly shine.
In trust, we find our sweetest grace,
Together, we can face this race.

Variables of Vulnerability

In shadowed corners, fears reside,
Yet in these depths, we learn to bide.
Vulnerability, a gift we bear,
Unveiling truths, learning to share.

With open hearts, we face the day,
Embracing flaws that come our way.
Each crack a door to deeper trust,
In honest moments, we must adjust.

We dance through storms, we find our way,
In fragile thoughts, we choose to stay.
For strength is found in every tear,
In showing up, we conquer fear.

So let us revel in our plight,
Acknowledging the dark and light.
In every scar, a story dwells,
In vulnerability, our spirit swells.

The Arithmetics of Ambivalence

Two paths diverge in muted light,
One whispers hope, the other, fright.
A dance of thoughts, a constant pull,
In shadows, doubts begin to lull.

Balance teeters on a thread,
With every choice, the heart is led.
Equations clash beneath the stars,
Chasing dreams, ignoring scars.

The weight of love in perfect sums,
Yet fear can echo, like distant drums.
In every sigh, a comma waits,
A heartbeat lost in twisting fates.

Proof of Existence

In quiet moments, echoes call,
A testament that we are all.
Among the noise, a whisper speaks,
In solitude, the spirit seeks.

Every breath, a mark in time,
A heartbeat's pulse, a subtle rhyme.
Our shadows stretch, both near and far,
Proof lies hidden in each scar.

In laughter shared and tears we shed,
In love that grows, in words unsaid.
Existence dances, light as air,
A fleeting touch, a fleeting care.

Solving for Heartstrings

In tangled threads of fate's design,
We search for answers, yours and mine.
Each glance a puzzle, each touch a clue,
What binds us close, yet feels so new.

An algebra of love's embrace,
Where variables can shift their place.
With every sigh, a question looms,
Unlocking joy from hidden rooms.

Through trials faced, we find the sum,
Of dreams united, fears undone.
Together solving longing's call,
The heartstrings strong, they will not fall.

Variables of the Soul

Amidst the chaos, stillness grows,
A journey deep where kindness flows.
With every turn, a choice unfolds,
The language of the heart is bold.

In every smile, a fragment gleams,
Reflecting hopes and shattered dreams.
Variables twist, yet seek to play,
In shadows cast by light of day.

Fragments gather, forming whole,
A tapestry that warms the soul.
Embrace the chaos, dance along,
For every note can join the song.

Multiplying Moments

In the quiet hush of dawn,
Time unfurls its gentle wings.
Each heartbeat counts, a quiet bond,
Whispers of what the future brings.

Memories dance like fleeting light,
Captured glances in the air.
Every moment holds its weight,
In a tapestry we share.

With laughter echoing through space,
We stitch our lives, thread by thread.
In the matrix of our days,
We find the dreams we've bred.

So let us multiply the joys,
Embrace each second, every change.
For in this vast and wondrous world,
The moments we make are never strange.

The Coefficient of Hope

Amidst the shadows, a light glows,
A number in an endless quest.
It shows us how the beauty grows,
In the equation of our rest.

With every struggle, every tear,
The sum of strength begins to rise.
In unity, we conquer fear,
Our dreams expand beyond the skies.

The variables of life conspire,
To spark a flame where darkness lay.
Hope's the constant, never tire,
In every battle, come what may.

So let's embrace this potent force,
With courage, passion, and intent.
For hope will chart our destined course,
A life of love and dreams well-spent.

Roots of Recollection

Beneath the surface, whispers dwell,
Stories hidden deep and wide.
Each memory, a fragile shell,
Guarding truths we often hide.

In twilight's glow, they start to bloom,
Old laughter mingles with the new.
The heart recalls a distant room,
Where shadows danced in shades of blue.

We dig through layers, find the past,
Like roots entwined, a sacred bond.
In moments shared, we are amassed,
For every journey carries fond.

So let us nurture these deep ties,
Celebrate what time has spun.
In the garden of our lives,
Recollection blossoms, never done.

Perpendicular Paths

Two lives intersect, a fleeting glance,
Destinies met on a line so bold.
Like arrows shot in a silent dance,
Each story unique, yet untold.

In crowded rooms, echoes of fate,
Where words collide with silent dreams.
Navigating time, we hesitate,
Caught in the web of hurried schemes.

Yet in the midst of chaos found,
A spark ignites, a pathway made.
Through fleeting moments, love is crowned,
Ours is a journey unafraid.

Though separate paths may lead us wide,
In the heart's compass, we are true.
For every crossing cannot hide,
The beauty born when paths renew.

Theorems of Trust

In shadows deep, we stake our claim,
With whispered fears and hidden flame.
Promises dance on fragile threads,
Bound by the hopes that love embeds.

Equation crafted with tender care,
Every secret shared, a breath of air.
From doubts that linger, we build and rise,
An algebraic bond beneath clear skies.

Proving the paths that lead us true,
In each theorem, I find you.
A synthesis formed from heart and mind,
In this math, your trust I find.

So let us weave this gentle art,
Each proof a canvas, painted heart.
Together we stand, two souls entwined,
In theorems of trust, our fate defined.

Sum of Secrets

In corners dark, where whispers lie,
We count the truths, we dare not try.
Each little secret, a piece of me,
Adding up slowly, can you see?

With every glance, a story shared,
In silence bound, we are declared.
The sum of moments, both light and shade,
In this equation, love is laid.

A ledger kept in hearts alone,
Balancing trust, a hidden tone.
Fractions of laughter, decimals of pain,
In sums of secrets, we're never the same.

What do we owe to what's unsaid?
The weight of silence, softly tread.
In every silhouetted stance,
The sum of secrets is our dance.

Rational Numbers in Chaos

In a world unruly, we seek our place,
With logic binding, we chase the grace.
Rational numbers, a line so neat,
In chaos swirling, they find their beat.

From fractions formed in hasty minds,
To integers lost in tangled binds.
Amidst the tumult, we draw a line,
Finding order where stars align.

Each calculation, a heartbeat true,
In a sea of madness, it's me and you.
Proportions steady, like tides that flow,
We'll grasp the logic in the throes of woe.

Through chaos and clamor, we sift and sort,
In rational numbers, we find our court.
Together we stand, in the storm we dwell,
In a dance of chaos, we weave our spell.

Intersection of Dreams

At twilight's edge, we pause and sigh,
Two dreams converge beneath the sky.
Paths that cross where wishes flow,
In the intersection, we dare to glow.

Colors blend in the dusky hue,
Your dream's a canvas, mine's the blue.
Together we sketch this world unknown,
In our fusion, seeds are sown.

A tapestry woven with threads of fate,
In this crossroads, it's never too late.
Every heartbeat whispers, 'This is real,'
The intersection of dreams we feel.

Let's wander through realms where visions gleam,
In the magic of night, we float and dream.
Together unbound, in the starlit seams,
We'll forever dance in the intersection of dreams.

The Matrix of Memories

In the frames of time we dwell,
Threads of laughter, whispers tell.
Captured moments, fleeting grace,
Memory's shadows softly trace.

Echoes linger in the night,
Fragments dance in silver light.
Each a story, deep and wide,
In the matrix, dreams abide.

Woven tales of love and loss,
Paths we take, the lines we cross.
With each heartbeat, memories grow,
In our minds, a vibrant glow.

Mosaic pieces, bright and dark,
In our souls, they leave a mark.
Together, they form our lore,
A tapestry forevermore.

Expressions of Existence

Life unfurls in vibrant hues,
Every moment stirs and brews.
Colors blend, we find our place,
In the chaos, we find grace.

Words can dance or softly sigh,
Underneath the endless sky.
Each expression, pure, profound,
Where our true selves can be found.

In the silence, voices rise,
Through the darkness, we will prize.
In the echoes of our heart,
Existence plays its rhythmic part.

Shared connections, hearts align,
In the universe, we entwine.
With each breath, we learn, we grow,
In existence, love will flow.

The Curvature of Past

Bowed and bent like silent trees,
Whispers carried on the breeze.
Tracing lines where shadows fall,
In the past, we learn it all.

Time is shaped by every choice,
In the stillness, hear our voice.
Curved horizons, endless routes,
Every journey has its doubts.

Fleeting moments, etched in time,
In the silence, there's a rhyme.
Curvature that leads us back,
To the essence we all lack.

Sketches of what used to be,
Holding fragments of the sea.
The curvature, a guiding path,
Through the echoes of our past.

The Derivatives of Dreams

In the night, our visions soar,
Fleeting thoughts, we all explore.
Dreams like rivers twist and bend,
Guiding us where hopes ascend.

Each derivative, a new start,
Whispers kindling in the heart.
Mathematics of our desire,
Chasing sparks, igniting fire.

Calculating paths unknown,
Through the darkness, we have grown.
In equations, we find our way,
Where tomorrow meets today.

Charting futures, bold and bright,
Within our dreams, we find our light.
The derivatives gently scheme,
Building worlds from every dream.

Multiplying Moments

In the quiet dawn's embrace,
Time ticks softly, like a tune.
Every second, a chance to trace,
Memories born beneath the moon.

Laughter dances, sparks ignite,
We weave our stories, bright and true.
In this tapestry of light,
Each moment shared, a vibrant hue.

In a world that swiftly spins,
We gather fragments, hold them near.
With every joy, each heart that wins,
Multiplying moments, crystal clear.

Through the years, we gently grow,
Nested dreams in time's embrace.
Each moment cherished, seeds we sow,
Harvesting love in this vast space.

Factors of Forgiveness

A heart divided, heavy weight,
Anger's fire can blind the way.
In silence, we contemplate,
The cost of letting hurt decay.

With gentle words, we seek to mend,
Understanding blooms like spring.
In the shadows, hearts can bend,
Factors of peace begin to sing.

In the dance of give and take,
We find the strength, the will to heal.
A spark of love, a chance we make,
Forgiveness born through every reel.

So we cast aside our pride,
And in this space, let kindness flow.
With open hearts, we stand beside,
The factors of love we come to know.

Coefficients of Connection

In every glance, a silent bond,
The universe conspires sweet.
Rays of warmth, a gentle wand,
Coefficients in love's heartbeat.

Through laughter shared, a tether formed,
An unseen thread that ties us tight.
In stormy weather, we've transformed,
Our spirits soaring, taking flight.

Every moment, a spark divine,
In conversations deep and true.
Together, we create the line,
Coefficients of me and you.

As seasons change, we're not alone,
Each connection, a guiding light.
In this garden, love has grown,
Coefficients hold us through the night.

The Symmetry of Affections

In every glance, a mirror's gaze,
Reflected warmth in love's design.
The gentle rhythm, tender ways,
Symmetry sparks, our hearts align.

In the quiet whispers shared,
Each word as soft as silken threads.
With every gesture, love declared,
Creating paths where kindness spreads.

Through trials faced and joy embraced,
Our souls entwined, a sacred dance.
In perfect harmony, interlaced,
Affections bloom, a timeless chance.

So let us cherish this sweet art,
The symmetry that binds us tight.
For in each other's beating heart,
Affections shine, our guiding light.

The Canvas of Connections

Upon this canvas, colors blend,
Fingers touch, and hearts extend.
Threads of laughter, whispers low,
In every stroke, our stories flow.

Moments shared like brushstrokes fine,
Every bond a careful line.
In shadows deep and light so bright,
We craft our art, we share our light.

Fragments weave in vibrant threads,
In silent joy, where love's heart treads.
Together, we create the space,
A masterpiece of time and grace.

The Sequence of Suffering

Deep within the heart's terrain,
Lies a path of silent pain.
Each step taken, heavy tread,
A story whispered, softly said.

Moments linger, time distorts,
Bearing burdens, life contorts.
Yet through the tears, the strength we find,
In shadows dark, a light defined.

We mend the cracks, we forge the steel,
In every wound, we learn to heal.
A sequence bound in human grace,
Through every trial, we embrace.

From ashes rise, the spirit's flight,
Resilient souls in endless fight.
In suffering's depth, love's bloom we see,
A tapestry of hope, endlessly free.

Constants in Chaos

In the tempest, voices clash,
Yet, still we find our peace, our stash.
Like stars that flicker in the night,
Guiding hearts to find what's right.

Through swirling winds and restless seas,
Lies a truth that sets us free.
A gentle hand, a soft embrace,
Amidst the chaos, we find our place.

The laughter heard above the noise,
Reminds us of our simple joys.
Anchored firm in love's bright glow,
Through every storm, our spirits grow.

Constants cherished, bonds so dear,
In life's wild dance, we persevere.
Chaos reigns, but love will stay,
A lighthouse shining through the gray.

Reflections in the Mirror

In glassy depths, a face appears,
Echoes soft, entwined with fears.
Each wrinkle tells a story old,
A journey rich, a life unfolds.

Moments captured, joy and pain,
In every glance, the lessons reign.
Reflections shift with time's embrace,
A changing view, a fleeting grace.

The eyes that meet, a silent plea,
To understand, to simply be.
In fractured light, our truths are found,
In mirrors deep, our souls unbound.

So look again, and see what's there,
A tapestry of hope, laid bare.
With every glance, a chance to grow,
Reflections teach us to let go.

The Geometry of Love

Love is a triangle, sharp at the tips,
Angles of passion, where kindness eclipses.
In a circle of warmth, we find our embrace,
Each curve a sweet whisper, no room for disgrace.

Lines crisscross in playful, tender dance,
Building connections, a heartfelt romance.
As shapes intertwine in heart's sacred space,
We sketch out our dreams, love's intricate lace.

In symmetry found, two hearts beat as one,
Uniting on paths, we race towards the sun.
Pythagorean proof that together we stand,
The geometry of love, perfectly planned.

So, measure your heart, let it freely steer,
In this vast equation, let go of your fear.
With formulas woven, attraction's embrace,
The beauty of love, a geometric grace.

Integer of Tears

In the quiet night, an integer sighs,
Each tear a whole number, pain never lies.
Counting emotions, the sum never ends,
Subtraction of laughter, the heart's heavy bends.

Each drop holds a story, a fraction of woe,
Adding to sorrow, where shadows still grow.
In the ledger of life, we tally our scars,
Dividing our joy by the light of the stars.

Through the prism of sadness, we gain some relief,
In integers fallen, we seek out belief.
Yet the value of love, though sometimes unclear,
Turns fractions to wholes, as we treasure each fear.

When eyes form equations and numbers collide,
We find in our tears, true love doesn't hide.
In the integer of tears, we learn to embrace,
Transforming our moments, through time and through space.

Subtracting Sorrows

In the silence of night, we weigh our regrets,
Subtracting the sorrows, as pain it begets.
With each passing moment, we learn to let go,
Finding solace in shadows, embracing the flow.

Negative thoughts linger, they cling like a vine,
But kindness can weed out, help hearts to entwine.
We add up the laughter, divide it by fear,
And gather the brightness, when loved ones are near.

The math of our hearts is complex yet clear,
Adding and subtracting, as we shed a tear.
For every lost moment, a lesson is found,
In the balance of kindness, our souls are unbound.

Our burdens grow lighter with each gentle breath,
Through love's perfect math, we conquer the death.
Subtracting our sorrows, we finally see,
The beauty of life, in a heart that is free.

The Paradox of Affection

In the chaos of hearts, affection we find,
A paradox woven, so gentle, yet blind.
It lifts us to heights, then drags us to ground,
Yet in sweet contradiction, our solace is found.

Fingers clasped tightly, yet the space can feel wide,
In love's tender embrace, we learn how to hide.
Through laughter and tears, a dichotomy we share,
The joy and the sorrow, a nuanced affair.

In vulnerability's depth, strength finds its way,
A dance of emotions, in night and in day.
With walls we erect, yet beckoning light,
The paradox of affection, our complex delight.

So cherish the blend of both joy and despair,
For in every heartbeat, we lay our hearts bare.
The paradox holds a beauty we've missed,
In love's sweet embrace, none can resist.

Inequalities of Desire

In the still of night, we roam,
Chasing dreams that feel like home.
Hearts collide, yet drift apart,
A puzzle missing every part.

Whispers linger on the breeze,
Promises made without a squeeze.
Hope can bloom in barren ground,
Yet thorns of doubt can still be found.

Desire dances, fickle flame,
A silent cry, yet never tame.
We reach for stars, but fall like rain,
The weight of longing brings us pain.

In shadows cast by fleeting light,
We seek the truth in endless night.
But in the dark, we learn to see,
Inequities of you and me.

The Calculus of Memories

In every moment, numbers play,
Calculating joy in shades of gray.
Memories flicker, a fleeting glance,
In equations lost, we yearn to dance.

Sum of laughter, the weight of tears,
Each fragment adds to what appears.
We graph the paths our lives have spun,
Intersecting fates, two minds as one.

Yet variables shift, time can skew,
The past feels strange, a faded hue.
Infinity loops in every choice,
In silence now, we feel the voice.

The calculus we try to hold,
A story written, yet untold.
In every theorem, we find the way,
To understand the price we pay.

Adding Up Regrets

Count the nights we stayed apart,
Each silence weighing on the heart.
The choices made, the words unspoken,
A chain of trust now left is broken.

Each moment lost, a bitter cost,
In shadows gathered, love is tossed.
We number chances like falling leaves,
In autumn's breath, our heart deceives.

But in the ledger of despair,
Some lines are bright, some marked by care.
A balance drawn with hope and pain,
In every loss, a hopeful gain.

As we add up what we regret,
We learn to love without the fret.
For in our sums, we find the grace,
To face the past and still embrace.

Subtracting Shadows

Beneath the weight of aching skies,
We strive to see through false goodbyes.
The fears that linger, pull us down,
But light can break through darkened frown.

We count the steps towards the dawn,
To find the strength to carry on.
Shadows stretch, then fade from sight,
As hope reclaims the lost, the light.

Subtract the doubts that cloud the mind,
In whispered truths, we seek to find.
A clearer path, a brighter way,
To chase the night and greet the day.

With every breath, we shed the past,
The echoes fade, the love will last.
Subtracting shadows, we emerge,
To find the life, anew we surge.

The Variables We Carry

Beneath our skins, numbers dwell,
Secrets we hold, stories to tell.
Each choice we make, a change unfolds,
The weight of our truths, precious like gold.

We measure our love in smiles and tears,
In laughter that echoes, through passing years.
The sum of our dreams, held close to the heart,
In this vast equation, we each play a part.

Balance of joy and sorrow entwined,
The variables shift, as life is designed.
Together we ride, on this tricky plane,
Finding our way through pleasure and pain.

A dance of complexity, each day we face,
With courage to carry, in this winding race.
No matter the odds, we resolutely stand,
In the realm of the variables, hand in hand.

Tensions of Togetherness

Threads woven tight in a tapestry bright,
Yet pull apart in the dead of night.
A shared glance that sparks, a gentle refrain,
In the tensions we face, there's growth from the pain.

Moments of silence, breaths held so near,
In the weight of the love, we also feel fear.
Misunderstandings, like shadows they loom,
Yet hope springs alive, evading the gloom.

Together we tangle, then untangle with grace,
In the dance of our hearts, we each find our place.
With laughter and conflict, we learn to embrace,
The tensions of love, our sacred space.

Through tempest and trial, our bond we renew,
In the delicate balance, we find something true.
For with every challenge, the fire burns bright,
In the tensions we hold, is the glory of light.

The Absolute Value of Vulnerability

In the softest of voices, truths come alive,
Barriers broken, we learn to survive.
To open our hearts, despite the great fear,
In the face of the storm, we find what is dear.

Each whisper of doubt is a chance to be bold,
In the nakedness found, our stories unfold.
The strength in our flaws, the power to heal,
In moments of loss, our spirits reveal.

Cradled in honesty, the beauty we find,
In the sharing of burdens, our souls intertwined.
We stand in our truth, stripped of pretense,
In the absolute value, we make recompense.

To be truly seen, a daunting feat,
Yet in this exposure, we find it complete.
With every soft click, the bonds we create,
In vulnerability's light, we illuminate fate.

The Geometry of Growth

Shapes of our journeys, angles we learn,
In twists and in turns, for wisdom we yearn.
Each step a new formula, paths intersect,
In the canvas of life, we build and connect.

Circles of trust, we learn to embrace,
Expand through the trials, gaining more space.
Triangles support, their strength we commend,
In the beauty of balance, our spirits ascend.

From points of departure, to lines that align,
In the equation of time, our paths intertwine.
In the depth of our roots, we rise and we soar,
The geometry of growth opens each door.

So let us embrace, all that we are,
In the shapes of our dreams, we reach for the stars.
With each growing angle, together we'll flow,
In the dance of existence, the seeds that we sow.

Balancing Love and Loss

In shadows deep, I find my way,
Your laughter lingers, night and day.
I cling to memories, soft and bright,
Yet fear the dark that steals my light.

A silent dance, we twirl and sway,
Between the love that fades away.
The echoes whisper, soft and clear,
Of all that was, and what we fear.

We navigate this fragile line,
Between the heartache and divine.
With every breath, I seek the grace,
To bless the love we can't replace.

Yet even with the heart's great ache,
I find the strength for love's own sake.
In loss, I learn, in love, I grow,
A journey paved with joy and woe.

The Coordinates of Comfort

In twilight's glow, our fingers touch,
A silent map, it tells so much.
The coordinates of where we've been,
Are sewn in moments, soft and thin.

Beneath the stars, our secrets lay,
In whispered dreams that drift away.
With every heartbeat, time's embrace,
We chart the paths, we dare to trace.

The warmth of you, my guiding star,
In every storm, no matter how far.
Our love's a compass, true and bright,
Leading us home, through darkest night.

Together we create a map,
In quiet places, a loving trap.
For in this world of chaos spun,
Your heart's my harbor, my only one.

The Science of Heartbeats

Two hearts aligned in rhythmic beat,
A subtle dance, love's pulse so sweet.
The science whispers in the air,
With every thump, we strip the bare.

Chemical bonds and neurons fire,
A spark ignites, an unquenched fire.
In frequencies of joy and pain,
We live the lessons love can train.

The rhythm swells, then fades away,
Yet in this silence, we still stay.
Our heartbeats speak a language rare,
Telling stories of love and care.

From tender touches to whispered sighs,
The science dwells where passion lies.
A lab of hearts, an open door,
In every heartbeat, we explore.

Unsolved Mysteries of Us

In riddles wrapped, our love remains,
A puzzle formed of joy and pains.
Each chapter written, every line,
A maze of moments, yours and mine.

With questions swirling, dreams unfold,
In corners dark, and truths untold.
We seek the answers, lost yet found,
In every heartbeat, love resounds.

The mysteries cling like stars at night,
In shadows deep, we search for light.
With every breath, we question more,
What lies beyond the open door?

In every glance, a world of clues,
An endless search that we must choose.
To solve the secrets deep inside,
Together we'll take this wild ride.

The Geometry of Grief

In shadows deep, I trace each line,
The angles sharp, where sorrow signs.
A heart's circumference, lost in time,
Each tear a point, where memories bind.

The space between, a hollow arc,
Defining loss, a silent mark.
Lines converge, where hopes once grew,
In solitude, I sketch what's true.

An open plane, where dreams once soared,
Now forms a path I can't afford.
The edges fray, the fabric wears,
In grief's geometry, no one cares.

Yet within this shape, a light may beam,
Transforming pain, igniting dreams.
For grief, though heavy, teaches grace,
In every angle, love finds its place.

Points of Intersection

Two lives entwined, a fleeting glance,
In crowded rooms, we took our chance.
Each laugh a spark, a shared delight,
In every heartbeat, paths ignite.

Yet time, it moves, with steady hand,
Divides the lines we once had planned.
In silence held, a sacred trust,
We find our way through love's robust.

Crossed wires, tangled in the dark,
Our whispered dreams, a tiny spark.
In moments brief, we chart the course,
Where shadows dance, we find the force.

Together still, despite the space,
In points of light, we find our grace.
With every turn, our paths align,
In intersections, love will shine.

The Integer of Whispers

In hushed confessions, numbers weave,
A tapestry of hearts that cleave.
Each digit soft, a truth to share,
In every silence, love does pair.

A count of sighs, in muted tones,
As secrets bloom, like hidden stones.
We share the sums of lives combined,
In equations formed, our souls entwined.

Integers rise, then fall away,
In whispered dreams, we find our say.
The math of hearts, both fierce and kind,
In every fraction, love's defined.

The whole of us, a pure delight,
In every whisper, burning bright.
With whispered words, the truth unfurls,
In integers, we change the worlds.

Expressing in Variables

In letters bold, our hearts define,
Each variable, a love aligned.
A whispered x, a yearning y,
Together crafting dreams on high.

We solve for joy, but fear the loss,
In every choice, we bear the cost.
Yet in the unknown, we find our way,
In every factor, hope will sway.

Each curve describes the paths we've crossed,
In every variable, we count the cost.
With every change, the numbers flow,
In chaos found, we learn to grow.

So let us write in equations clear,
With courage bold, and hearts sincere.
For love's the answer, pure and true,
In variables, we will break through.

The Dynamics of Desire

In the heart, whispers collide,
A dance of longing, side by side.
Chasing shadows in the night,
Fading dreams, out of sight.

Fractured hopes, yet we strive,
Through the chaos, we survive.
Yearning flames, they ignite,
Passion's spark, burning bright.

Every glance, a silent plea,
Entangled souls, wild and free.
The pull of fate, a sweet demand,
Together we explore the land.

In the ebb and flow, we find,
The heart's compass, ever blind.
With every turn, we discover,
What it means to truly love her.

The Reciprocity of Resilience

In the face of storms, we stand tall,
With broken wings, we rise from the fall.
Each bruise a lesson, each scar a tale,
In unity's arms, we shall not pale.

Together we weather, hand in hand,
Building bridges across the land.
Lifting spirits, a chorus of hope,
In the dark, we learn to cope.

Fragile hearts, yet fiercely bold,
In the heat of struggle, courage unfolds.
We share the weight as we ascend,
In resilience, we find our blend.

With whispers of strength, we ignite the spark,
Creating light in times so dark.
United we flourish, entwined in grace,
A tapestry woven, in this embrace.

Evaluating Emotions

In the mirror, feelings unfold,
A reflection of stories told.
Joy dances lightly on the skin,
While sorrows linger deep within.

Navigating the waves, we sail,
Charting paths where tempests wail.
Each moment a lesson, profound and raw,
We learn to love, we learn to claw.

Caught in the web of choice and chance,
We ponder, we pause, a wistful glance.
Heartbeats quicken, then slow their song,
In the balance, where we belong.

Through trials faced and victories gained,
We harvest wisdom, unrestrained.
In the tapestry of life's design,
We find the threads of heart entwined.

Cubic Complications

In corners sharp, shadows play,
Lost in dimensions, we drift away.
Layers of doubt, encased in fear,
Within the box, the world is near.

Thoughts entangled, a puzzling maze,
Seeking meaning in the haze.
Each twist, a turn, a fresh debate,
Cubic structures we create.

Voices echo in the void,
In measured steps, we are buoyed.
Solutions lurk in hidden lines,
Finding hope where chaos entwines.

With every edge, we dare to dream,
Challenging the norm, we scheme.
In the cube of life, unpredictable,
We navigate paths, unstoppable.

Algebra of the Unsaid

In whispers soft, the truth remains,
Equations written in shadowed gains.
Variables dance on the edge of dreams,
Silent answers echo in muted screams.

A fraction of hope in a sea of doubt,
Calculations hidden, waiting to sprout.
In every glance, a theorem unfolds,
The language of hearts, not easily told.

Complexity hides in the simple gaze,
Formulas crafted in unspoken ways.
Each sigh a symbol, each pause a line,
Solving the mysteries that intertwine.

Together, we solve this beautiful mess,
In algebra's arms, we find our finesse.
Though words may falter, the heart will stay,
In the silence, love finds its way.

Roots of Resilience

Through storms that rage and winds that howl,
We stand firm, like trees, strong and foul.
Deep in our souls, the roots run wide,
Nurtured by trials we do not hide.

Branches may sway, but we do not break,
Each struggle we face makes us awake.
In the rising sun, our spirits renew,
Finding the strength in shedding the blue.

From cracks in the earth, wildflowers bloom,
Amidst the grey skies, we seek out the room.
With every setback, we rise from the ground,
In the garden of hope, our strength is found.

Together we grow, side by side,
In the landscape of life, joy is our guide.
Resilience flows through every vein,
Rooted in love, we embrace the pain.

The Undefined Limits of Love

In the cosmos vast, our hearts collide,
Like stars that shimmer, we cannot hide.
Love knows no bounds, no set design,
Infinite angles where spirits align.

A dance of souls in the twilight glow,
Bound by an energy only we know.
In every heartbeat, a universe swells,
Where deep understanding perpetually dwells.

Undefined limits, we draw our lines,
In the canvas of life, where love entwines.
Each moment a brushstroke, vibrant and true,
Creating a masterpiece, just me and you.

Together we wander, lost in the night,
Charting the course to the edge of light.
For love is a journey, forever unframed,
In the galleries of time, we'll be named.

Charts of Change

Lines and graphs tell a story unclear,
Mapping the shifts that draw us near.
In every curve, a lesson appears,
Telling of hopes and of conquered fears.

The x-axis stretches, time moves along,
In the symphony of life, we find our song.
Peaks of joy, valleys of pain,
A tapestry woven in sunshine and rain.

Each data point a moment we seize,
Learning the flow, embracing the breeze.
From chaos to order, we find our way,
In the patterns of change, we choose to stay.

So let the charts guide where we roam,
For in every shift, we build our home.
Embracing the journey, forever engaged,
In the story of life, we are all page.

Patterns of Longing

In the quiet of the night, I see,
Whispers calling out to me.
They trace the edges of my dreams,
Fleeting shadows, silent themes.

With every breath, a wish returns,
A candle flickers, softly burns.
In every corner, hope resides,
Where heartache lingers, love abides.

The stars above begin to wane,
Yet still I bear the weight of pain.
In every thought, a soft embrace,
Patterns of longing, time won't erase.

So I gather all my threads,
Weaving stories, unspoken words.
In tangled twines, my heart's design,
A tapestry of love divine.

The Density of Doubts

Fading whispers fill the air,
Questions linger everywhere.
In shadows thick, true thoughts are lost,
Weighing heavily, at what cost?

In every choice, a mirror shows,
Reflections of the fear that grows.
Clouds of worry, thick and low,
A labyrinth where I dare not go.

The echoes of my inner fight,
Drift like fog, obscuring light.
Yet through the doubt, a spark ignites,
A tiny flame in darkest nights.

Though burdens coil around my heart,
I seek the strength to tear apart.
To find the path amidst the haze,
And turn my fears to brighter days.

The Angle of Affection

A glance exchanged beneath the moon,
The world reduced to just this tune.
In subtle smiles, our stories blend,
In every moment, love transcends.

With gentle touch, we build a bridge,
Every heartbeat, a sacred pledge.
In laughter shared, in silence, too,
The angle bends in shades of blue.

Through twisted paths, we find our way,
In every dawn, a bright display.
Our souls entwined, a dance of grace,
A tender touch, a warm embrace.

As seasons change and time moves fast,
In the angle of affection, we'll last.
For every challenge, hand in hand,
Together strong, we take our stand.

Refractions of Resolve

Through prisms bright the light does break,
Shadows formed, choices we make.
In every hue, a truth revealed,
The strength within, no longer concealed.

On shaky ground, foundations found,
In uncertainty, our hearts are bound.
A flicker of courage cuts the night,
Leading us to the edge of light.

In fragments scattered, hope takes shape,
A tapestry of dreams we drape.
With every step, the echoes call,
Refractions of resolve, we stand tall.

Though storms may brew and fears may rise,
In the depth of struggle, we find the prize.
For in the heart of every trial,
We gather strength, we learn to smile.

Asymptotes of Connection

In shadows we linger, reaching out,
A dance on the edge, filled with doubt.
We grasp for a moment, yet never quite hold,
Two lines converging, a story untold.

Time slips away, yet feelings remain,
A curve of affection, a beautiful pain.
We chase the horizon, we're close, yet apart,
Asymptotes of love, drawn from the heart.

With whispers of longing, we yearn for embrace,
Our paths intertwining, a fleeting trace.
In silence we speak, with each tender glance,
Two souls in the night, lost in the dance.

As stars blend with shadows, we find our way,
Navigating the space, both fragile and gay.
In this vastness we wander, forever sustained,
By asymptotes of connection, love's sweet refrain.

Tangents to Happiness

A fleeting moment, joy's sweet grace,
We seek the laughter, the light on our face.
Through curves of our journey, we find our place,
In tangents to happiness, life's warm embrace.

We chase the bright glimmers, the spark of delight,
In mundane routines, we find pockets of light.
With smiles shared freely, connections ignite,
A symphony playing, so joyous and bright.

Through ups and downs, our paths may diverge,
Yet happiness lingers, a constant urge.
We clasp each moment, let our hearts surge,
In tangents to joy, love's gentle merge.

In echoes of laughter, we build up our dreams,
With every connection, or so it seems.
In the tapestry woven, through life's flowing streams,
We find tangents to happiness, woven in beams.

The Sum of Us

In numbers we gather, a collective embrace,
Each heartbeat a rhythm, a dance in this space.
The joys and the burdens, all woven in trust,
Together we blossom, for we're the sum of us.

Through trials we stand, hand in hand, side by side,
With love as our anchor, we take every stride.
In laughter we flourish, in tears we adjust,
With dreams intertwining, we're the sum of us.

Like stars in the night, a constellation bright,
Each story a spark, illuminating the night.
In unity's strength, we rise from the rust,
Creating a future, for we're the sum of us.

In moments of silence, or joy that combusts,
In all of our journeys, love's magic we trust.
For in every heartbeat, in life's endless thrust,
Together forever, we're the sum of us.

Dimensions of Delight

In realms of the heart, where colors abide,
We paint with our laughter, with joy as our guide.
In each vibrant moment, our spirits take flight,
Exploring the layers, in dimensions of delight.

Through fields of soft blossoms, we wander and roam,
Finding the treasures that bring us back home.
In dances of sunshine and dreams taking flight,
We weave a rich tapestry, dimensions of delight.

In echoes of music, our souls intertwine,
With rhythms uplifting, in harmony's line.
Each heartbeat a brushstroke, painted so bright,
Creating a canvas, of dimensions of delight.

With open hearts bared, we savor the now,
In gentle affirmations, we silently vow.
For life is a journey, in love's purest light,
Exploring together, in dimensions of delight.

Inequalities of Desire

In shadows long, we reach for light,
A yearning heart, in silent night.
The dream is bright, yet snatched away,
Desires pull us, lead astray.

Hope's ember glows, with tender care,
Yet fears of loss, linger in air.
We chase the flames, with hands so bare,
A fragile bond, so hard to bear.

The Calculus of Change

Numbers dance in shifting sands,
Equations frame our restless hands.
Each moment's pulse, a variable,
In graphs of time, we find our soul.

Derivatives of joy and pain,
The limit approaches, yet we strain.
To find that point, we strive and seek,
In every loss, in every peak.

Finding X in Heartache

An unknown value, lost in tears,
We search for answers through the years.
Each heartbreak writes a story vast,
In quest for peace, we face the past.

Algebra of love, misaligned,
We graph the scars that fate designed.
Yet through the hurt, we learn to grow,
In solving X, we find our flow.

The Constant of Compassion

In every heart, a tender thread,
A warmth that flows, where hope is spread.
Compassion wakes the weary soul,
It binds us close, it makes us whole.

Through storms of life, we lend our hands,
Together strong, like shifting sands.
In shared embrace, we find our way,
A constant light in shades of gray.